Bouncing Back

Bouncing Back

Handling the Transition from Firing to the Next Job

Michael T. McCraley

Writers Club Press

San Jose New York Lincoln Shanghai

Bouncing Back
Handling the Transition from Firing to the Next Job

Writers Club Press
an imprint of iUniverse.com, Inc.

For information address:
iUniverse.com, Inc.
620 North 48th Street, Suite 201
Lincoln, NE 68504-3467
www.iuniverse.com

ISBN: 0-595-09945-9

Printed in the United States of America

DEDICATION

This book is dedicated to Marla, my understanding wife of over 30 years, who had to put up with several of my "transitions" during which I reorganized every closet and drawer in the house.

And...

To my daughter, Tracy,
who never really knew what I did for a living but
who always gave me her full support and more than
a few pep talks along the way.

I can only wish that those of you
who read this book receive the same amount of support that I did.

CONTENTS

INTRODUCTION

Having gone through downsizing, being fired and firing myself, I felt a need to walk other middle managers and senior executives through this highly emotional roller coaster ride. This book of short essays is intended to provide insights into the inner sanctum of one's thoughts during this time, send several well intentioned verbal kicks in the butt to the "transitioner" and offer significant doses of positive reinforcement to those facing this life altering experience.

Most of us, outside of doctors, lawyers and self-employed contractors will be faced with the reality of being out of a job sometime in our lives, especially if one is in the High Technology Industry.

Hopefully, this book helps ground "newcomers" to the reality of the process, takes away the mystery of what has happened and opens one's eyes to the opportunity that this unplanned event presents.

You can read this book in a single sitting, but you might want to take it in smaller doses as it is intended to provoke introspection and constructive self-evaluation.

Good Luck! Take the time to truly enjoy the experience that you are going through!

SECTION 1

AFTER THE SMOKE CLEARS, FIRST IMPRESSIONS

Been There....

How many times do you pick up the "how to" book on virtually any subject, read it cover to cover and take copious notes? You feel you are receiving the pearls of wisdom from the expert for only $19.95. Then you start the project only to find that one thing after another doesn't work the way it was advertised or doesn't make sense at all.

How can this be?

Returning to the book, you check out the book jacket to see what the background of the author is, only to find out that he is a full time professor with no real world experience in the topic he wrote the book about. It all came from other books probably written by the same type of academic with little or no appreciation of the real world.

The last thing you want now is to pick up a book on coping with the transition between jobs written by someone who never had a gap in his or her career.

Well—this is your lucky day!

I got my high school diploma, college degree and PHD in "transition".

Not only that but I was flexible in my sabbaticals with one from a start-up, one from a major Japanese company and one from a U.S. based multinational high tech company!

I have definitely been there and done that. I have a good appreciation for how you feel.

By the way, the higher one is in a company, doesn't make it any more palatable (contrary to what some newspaper editorial writers suggest).

Look at this book as a series of stream-of-conscious thoughts about the ultimate downer, the time between jobs. Latch on to those thoughts that best help you work through it.

OH MY! WHAT A SURPRISE!

Never in a million years did you think that it would happen to you.

You worked hard. You always brushed your teeth and took showers daily. You even went to church on Sundays.

That wasn't the problem.

The truth of the matter is that you didn't tune into what changes were going on around you in the company, in the industry and, in many cases, in your own department. You even thought "out of sight, out of mind" was a good way to run your daily routine in your job.

What you did was make yourself expendable. Without high profile connections in the industry (in a technical or business sense), without any mentor in your division, department or section, you were the walking unknown.

It's easy to cut people without identity, people without power and definitely people without friends in high places.

It pays to network as much when you are working as it is a necessity when you are on the street "in transition". Keep involved.

There should never be a surprise firing. We all should know if we are doing a good job or not. Our being asked to be part of special projects, our annual reviews, and our ability to get others to follow our lead or agree with us. There are hundreds of signs that tell us whether we are on the up curve or on the down curve.

Take that thought to the bank or to the employment office.

How Many Ways Can You Say "Fired"?!

Downsized, rightsized, outsourced, resized, laid off, terminated, made redundant, transitioned out, position closed, etc. etc.

Any way you say it, you no longer have a job.

Time to get used to this reality and get on with finding your next job.

You probably knew it was coming but did not want to admit it to yourself since you come from the old school of "work hard and you have a job for life".

That is still true.

Just that the definition of life has changed a lot. Now it may mean the life of a project, life of your manager, life of your product, life after takeover.

THE THEORY OF INDISPENSABILITY

If you are reading this book, you have already discovered the basic flaw in the Theory of Indispensability.

No matter how experienced you are, how many years you have with the company, how technically competent, you are replaceable. That is, unless you are the relative of the owner or President of the company.

But that is another story.

Starting in the 80's and growing to epidemic proportions in the 90's, corporations began the game of buyouts and the resultant pruning of redundant functions that would promise the financial health of the new combined entity.

The age of looking at numbers, rather than individual people as the foundation for a successful business, is now the norm.

So, what do you do now that you have become aware of this fact of life, firsthand?

First, admit that it is a fact and then get on with your life.

From now on, you should look at yourself as a temporary contractor. As such, you have to make things happen every day that starts paving the way for the future job, either in your present company or in the outside world at company "X".

This even means that you have to change the way you look at retirement. As an independent contractor, you will need to develop an investment strategy based on your own investing rather than counting on company retirement programs. Don't get lulled into thinking things are different just because you get a job with a nice corner office and an executive secretary.

Times have changed.

READ ANY HANDWRITING
ON THE WALLS LATELY?

It's there if you stand back from your day to day activities and look at the big picture.

Business is moving at an ever increasing rate in making decisions on people, new equipment purchases, acquisitions, de-acquisitions etc. These changes send out signals just like a bat "sounding" to avoid hitting walls when it flies.

Watch for the red flags. Here are a few of my favorites. Looking back, I am sure you can think of your own red flags now that the initial shock of your dismissal has worn off and you have moved from severe manic-depressive to merely angry.

RED FLAG EXAMPLES:

—New boss hires on and he starts to hire "his team". Read this as "you are now the old team". Guess what happens to the old team?

—New boss of the boss (i.e. Group VP, Group President): He/she often has a godfather in the parent company and he/she is on a mission (not the Mormon kind). His first acts are to prove his worth. So expect changes, mostly dramatic and very highly visible in order to score points with his manager.

—Major reorganization announcement that affects your department which you were not previously privy to. Big problem here. This is a 3 alarm red flag! Time to get out the resume because no help is on the way.

—Your boss takes a sudden interest in your travel plans combined with his announcing special meetings that happen to

fall during the time you are traveling. And you are excused from having to attend due to the travel. A little suspicious I would say. —Final example is one where you are in charge of sales. Sales are weak due to poor quality and product obsolescence while your competition is selling "plug and play" highly reliable products and has introduced new products that are 30% faster than anything you have to sell. However, raising these facts with your boss is looked at as adversarial and he additionally questions your sales skills during such meetings. This is a real killer if this is the new boss and the heads of engineering and manufacturing (sources of poor quality and lack of new products) are "his" guys while you are the "old" team.

Regardless of the scenario, the fact is that such handwriting is always on the wall.

You need to be tuned into these clues to avoid being caught unawares. With some warning, you may be able to counteract your company's perception of you. Or, in the worst case, set in motion your plan for your next job before the axe officially comes down.

Never Burn Bridges

We've all heard the phrase, "never burn bridges" but never will this concept have more meaning than during the layoff or firing process.

At that moment of your business career, you are carrying the most emotional baggage. Your frustration level is at its highest point and your desire to shoot first and ask questions later is greatest.

It is time to revisit your early bible readings especially where the phrase "turn the other cheek" was quoted, because this is the time that you will have the most urgent need to invoke this bit of advice. Your best bet is to contain yourself for the moment and make a quick trip to the gym for a long and exhausting workout.

What you don't realize, now in the heat of your dismissal, is that you will run across the same people in the future that you want the most to lambaste today. It is understandable with all of the frustrations that have built up during your employment that you want to release this venom at the time of departure.

More interesting is the fact that in this future meeting with your former boss/associate, they will again be in positions of authority, and you will need their help or business. I realize that this is hard to believe in the heat of the moment.

This advice is for real, especially in this fast paced economy.

Don't burn bridges when you leave.

In fact, use this situation as an opportunity to take advantage of the vulnerability of the person doing the firing to elicit a reference for a next job or a better exit package.

This seems a perverse idea until you have gone through a few reorganizations and find that no one is irreplaceable. In fact, you will

also find that the person doing the firing is having as tough a time doing the firing as you are feeling on the receiving end. In fact, he/she is feeling so bad that he/she is open to honor-saving actions to make himself or herself feel better. This is the ideal time to ask for additional severance pay, outplacement help and extension of benefits, use of cell phone and on and on.

When you leave in a classy way, this professionalism under duress goes a long way to give you bonus points down the road from those directly and indirectly involved in your departure.

Release of anger feels good only for the moment but the fallout will last a lifetime.

SECTION 2

SEARCH ISSUES/ HINTS/THOUGHTS

THE GAME—HOW TO PLAY

One concept you won't often hear is that the transition process is a game.

Surprise! The transition process is as much a game as musical chairs or, should I say, missing chairs that got you here in the first place. There are rules and winners and losers just like every other game. Most people never think of the transition process this way and miss the fun part.

I don't mean to trivialize your situation at all, only to put it into a perspective that allows you to realize that getting that next job is going to be a game, not of fancy, but of wits, endurance, patience and survival.

You are now entering into a competition with numerous unnamed and unknown rivals that will end many times without your knowledge and without any reason as to why you didn't finish in the top 3 finalists or as the winner. In this game, no person feels obligated to keep the others informed.

Rather diabolical, isn't it?

In this game, you are a one-man team that has to call on the resources of others, a.k.a. the infamous network of friends and business acquaintances, to solicit hints as to the "best way" to do a variety of things, from introductions to thank you notes.

It can be an exciting game. It is definitely a full time game where research, cold calling, persistence, introspection and flexibility are key to being successful.

If you enjoy games, then look at this as being the "big one". The process can be fun and will definitely force you to realize that there are a lot more options than just bouncing into another job of the kind that you just left. For me, I am writing, consulting, investigating the purchase

of my own business (including a vineyard) and also investigating joining a major company.

Maybe I will do all of that. Maybe I won't. But I sure feel that I have a lot more in me to offer than in the job that I left.

I am a powerful dude and so are you. So let's get on with the game!

Setting Priorities

Simple as 1, 2, 3. That is what priority setting is.

You recognize that first of all, you are not God and never will be (I may lose this argument with some of you but.). Only God can do everything simultaneously with equal success. For us humans, we are limited to keeping at best 4-6 balls (projects) in the air at one time. So we must find a way to prioritize what we are doing and then get on with dealing with the prioritized projects.

A simple way to prioritize is to pick the top 3-4 projects with either the greatest payback or greatest global impact on your search.

This seems so obvious when we were running our businesses (if it isn't obvious, that may be one reason why you are out here reading this book). It should also be obvious in running your new job or finding yourself a new job.

First and foremost, you must do a thorough self-analysis to define your strengths and weaknesses. Then define where you want to go based on your business background, your interests, skills and strengths. Finally, set up a strategic plan outlining your actions to achieve the goal of snagging the new job. This is a simple description of a very time consuming process.

The point to be made is that the job hunting process must be attacked in a systematic and highly prioritized manner just like the successful projects that you ran in your previous job.

Looking is Harder than Working

You are reading this book, having just been laid off.

And you are saying to yourself, "hey, this isn't too bad. I don't have to get up early to shave and dress up, let alone take that two hour commute to work".

"Besides this, I won't have to deal with that SOB (fill in the blank). Now, I can catch up on some reading, get my golf game in shape and visit wine country".

This assumes that you either got a nice severance package or have a nice bank account to lean back on.

STOP THAT THINKING RIGHT NOW!

The situation you are in today is not a vacation. In fact, the work that will be required to get you that new job will probably be harder than actually working. Sort of like the way the old Green Bay Packers under Vince Lombardi use to describe their practices versus the actual game day. They had been worked so hard during the practices that the Sunday game was almost like a day off.

Well, you have now entered the same situation.

You have a lot of work to do.

You need to do a self-assessment, compile a list of friends and business acquaintances for networking, put together a resume, plan your strategy for what companies and industry you want to target for your next job and then get the word out to all of those people via e-mail, fax, letter, phone and face-to-face meetings.

Buddy, you have a lot of work to do!

Believe me, being out of the mainstream, you are quickly forgotten and your skills erode fast unless constantly exercised, just like your muscles.

You must structure your day as though you are in a real job, the only difference being that now you are selling yourself instead of a widget. This is not an easy task because, for many of you, you haven't had to sell yourself for many years. For us experienced types, it is a little easier, but not much.

Let me jolt you into the reality of what you are facing. You will be spending a lot of time contemplating this little fact in the coming months.

Your job search will take approximately one month for every $10,000 increment in salary you expect to earn.

Don't believe, even in a hot market, statistics in the papers pointing to an average time of 3-4 months to land a job. Those numbers are misleading in that they group together a broad spectrum of jobs at all levels. So a janitor is lumped with a VP slot. There is a big difference in the time to find a job as you go up the food chain.

In summary, the harder one works getting the next job, the sooner it becomes a reality.

SEVERANCE IS A SUBSIDIZED EDUCATION NOT A VACATION

Aha! You're one of the lucky ones whose company gave a severance package to when you parted from their employment.

Severance comes in all shapes and terms, from as little as the unused vacation time due to a package based on a ratio of weeks or months of salary for every year worked. Every once in a while, one is able to lock up a guaranteed severance that is much longer due to the executive job level. Or, guaranteed severance is provided due to the volatility of the position. Such severance guarantees are the only way one would take the job in the first place.

In any case, a few words of caution:

—Rather than taking a lump sum payment, take the payment over time just like regular salary. This does two things for you. It keeps your income steady and more importantly, it allows you to continue your medical and health care benefits at the lower company rate instead of having to pay for these costs under a Cobra plan (some 2-3 times more expensive).

—Never look at severance time as a vacation. It is at best a subsidized job hunt or educational sabbatical.

It is tempting to go on vacation to forget the whole ugly mess. FORGET IT!

Your funds are finite. The job market is unpredictable. And time goes way too fast when you combine these two facts.

Instead of working on solving problems at a company, you are now a full time member of YOU Inc. Your full time job is to get YOU Inc. back to

work. And understand that YOU Inc.'s cash flow is negative. Severance is a subsidy for this process.

This is the time to get the education that will help in your next career. Brush up on accounting, take computer software lessons on new networking programs, and catch up on reading on key trade press in your targeted industry. Set your daily calendar to work these things in.

If nothing else, you no longer have to worry about those silly business meetings and reports to interrupt what you are doing.

Plan that vacation as a reward when you get the next job.

Keeping In Shape

When you are working fifteen-hour days and sometimes six and seven-day weeks, especially when you travel a lot, your body is being severely stressed.

Without some form of regular exercise, you will find that gravity is increasingly winning the war.

Your Michelin tire, where your trim waist used to be, is now inflating and your energy is dropping off in direct proportion. Sooner or later, something has to give. Heart attacks, high blood pressure and stress induced illnesses can become a reality.

Now that the job is no longer taking up all your time, it is a great time to do something about your health.

This transition period is actually a bonus in that you can initiate a "new you" program of exercise and diet that can get you back in shape and keep you there when you start your next job. Starting such a program is not only helpful for increasing your longevity, but it is critical in giving you some sorely needed self confidence and self esteem in this emotionally trying transition period between jobs.

You need all the energy you can sum up to keep a positive attitude. Getting your body in shape will give you that energy and an extra boost of "tude" to carry you through the ebb and flow of the job hunting process. The only downside maybe the havoc your new body creates with your clothing budget. That and learning how to handle those admiring glances.

Remember back when you were hiring to fill an open position in your department? What impressed you about the different people who were trying to get the job besides their experience and expertise? Most

likely you unconsciously or consciously felt more positive toward people who were high energy, carried themselves well, appeared in good health and were professional in appearance.

Look in the mirror and see if you would hire yourself based on the criteria that you used to judge others.

Believe me, those on the other side of the desks will be making such judgements.

GETTING TO KNOW AT&T UP FRONT AND CLOSE

One of the real winners in the transition process is AT&T (to say nothing of Sprint, MCI etc.).

These people and their equipment will become real familiar to you during this period. A bonding takes place after the 50th or 60th call. You now appreciate for the first time why other people speak so longingly about the old Ma Bell and how simple things used to be.

Now access codes and calling card numbers make "let your fingers do the walking through the yellow pages" seem like child's play. A phone keypad becomes a virtual typewriter with all the keystrokes one is required to type. This is amplified when you hit the jackpot of voicemail systems where they ask you to pull up the employee directory and spell out "Grudliexhskyzi", your contact name, using the keypad.

However, the reality is that you will need to take advantage of the phone for multiple uses now as never before.

For practical purposes, be sure to get an additional 1-2 phone lines installed in your home office. This allows you to send/receive faxes, connect to the Internet via a modem and have a private business-only line to insure privacy and quality time for someone who is calling you regarding a potential new position.

Sitting in the kitchen on the family phone while the TV is blaring and the dishes are being done will only help your chances if you are seeking a 3rd shift cooks job.

The upside to all this is that these expenses are tax deductible and you get special discounted rates for the service you are adding. Hey, if you work the system just right, you can even earn frequent flyer miles to use when you take that pre-job vacation.

NETWORKING

This is one of those overworked words that really does have merit, especially in the context of those in the transition process.

This concept is about as fundamental to your future success as can be, whether you are in the transition process or actively engaged in a career. It is the stuff by which careers are launched, businesses are conceived and relationships are started.

Networking is simply the act of broadening your network of business and personal relationships via a proactive seeking out of new contacts by way of those you presently know.

An example would be your wife playing tennis with the wife of a president of a company in an unrelated industry. You are introduced to this person and find a common need that you can resolve. Just such an unplanned connection resulted in my changing industries and moving into the world of Robotics.

The foundation of good networking is that it is a two way street, not an opportunity to sponge off another person or take advantage of their generosity in helping a total stranger out of a problem. Such networks are to be used on a continuing basis to reinforce their longevity and utility to both parties. Daily calls are not needed but timely periodic updates are a must.

Mr. Millikan of stock market fame had a network of thousands that he regularly contacted via a phone call or a short note. Not sure how much this helped him during his trial, but I think you understand the concept. Knowledge is power and networking is the art of building a power base of relationships in all aspects of your business and personal life.

For an "executive in waiting" such as you, embracing this concept will be the greatest "take away" you may get from this book on the transition process.

YOU MUST INITIATE NETWORKING, if you don't already do it! And, you must keep it active beyond using it only in a time of need such as now.

How to start is easier than you might think. Get out several pieces of paper and merely list everyone you know from a personal friend to a business acquaintance. You will quickly come up with a list of in excess of 300-400 names. As you think further about it, many more names will come to mind.

However, this first list is your starting network. You know these people for various reasons, peers at work, members of a neighborhood association, neighbors, golfing buddies and on and on.

Now what you want to do is to find a reason for contacting them again in such a way that will allow you to build the relationship.

For instance, informing them that you are in transition and are looking for a little direction on a certain element of your search. Or asking them to give you benefit of their ideas or a name of someone who they think will help. Asking for help is a powerful enabler in itself. It is flattering to be asked. And you will find assistance coming freely.

You can see how this process can quickly build a new network of references over time. And, through it all, you are not putting these contacts on the spot. You are only giving them the opportunity to give some advice. In return, you can offer them contacts in your industry or personal references from your vast network.

This is what I call a legally ethical Ponzi scheme.

As an executive, you have been doing this all your life without thinking about it. Now, you are formalizing the process. Let technology help you out and compile these contacts into a relational data base to be called upon at will in the future as different needs arise.

You will find networking to be one of the most powerful tools for your search and your career after the search is successfully completed. At a minimum, this active communication reconnects you to that outside world that you have most recently exited.

It is good therapy.

It is a great process.

Good Luck!

Never Say Never (at Work & to Headhunters)

Never, Never, Never, Never, Never, Never, Never, say "Never"!

Never, Never, Never say it to a headhunter even when you are happily entrenched in a fantastic job!

"Why" you ask? Well, the simple fact is that your fantastic job may disappear in a nanosecond (faster than you can react, believe me). The headhunter may be your lifeline.

As for your boss, your positive response to new requests makes you a "keeper" when times get tough and the company needs to list the top ten candidates for the twilight zone. However, this may not save you if the mandated number of twilight zone candidates exceeds the list of "disposables". In that case, you may still become the unfortunate target of the hit list. (For reference sake, you should note that your boss will be the last to go even if the department disappears below him). So—when he requests volunteers for jobs, you should be quick to respond to keep your name on the "keeper" list.

The biggest 'yes" you can do is to make sure that you treat those headhunters who call with the utmost courtesy. If you are out of town, answer when you get back or within 24 hours after retrieving voice mail. Even if you have no interest in the position he/she is inquiring about, be prepared to pass along several potential candidates from your network. These people might be candidates or give references to others who may be candidates.

Always make sure that the person you reference knows you and that this headhunter uses your name to explain how their name was referenced. This tactic accomplishes two things. It tells those that you referenced that you still are thinking of them for good positions. And it

tells the headhunter that you are a valuable resource for their searches. You also get plus marks in the headhunter's books when the right job for you crosses his desk in a future search.

In both cases, you are now put on the list of the good guys. This will pay off down the road.

Keep those phone lines and references active.

LOOK IN THE MIRROR

Every day before you used to head to the office, you probably did the same routine: shave (optional on women), shower, put on your suit, eat breakfast and brush your teeth just like the dentist recommends.

Before leaving the house, you took that last look in the mirror to make sure everything was in place, tie straightened, suit collar down, no lint on the jacket and shoes shined.

This is the routine that we all took for granted as the norm and as the best way to start the day whether at home or while traveling on business.

Now that you no longer have a job, the look in the mirror is slightly different. Now it means the total and brutally honest reappraisal of your strengths and weaknesses. This reappraisal is what is needed to get you in shape for the next job.

This could mean going on a diet, starting an exercise program, taking those long delayed computer courses at the local college or going back to school full time to get your undergraduate or masters degree.

The bottom line is putting yourself together in such a way as to be the best candidate for your next step in your career.

To get there is going to require you to do a thorough self audit or to go to a third Party counselor who can help you do this through the use of tests on skill sets, personality profiles and recommendations of jobs based on the results of the tests.

Looking in the mirror is a great first step to develop the winning combination for your next job.

COLD WEEKS/HOT DAYS

You have been terminated and you are out looking for that next great job.

You have generated a masterpiece of a resume and have sent this resume to every retained search consultant that you found in the latest edition of John Lucht's **Rites of Passage** or The **Directory of Executive Recruiters**. In the process, you have gotten to know the manager of the Quik Copy franchise on a first name basis.

You have contacted all your friends to advise them of your career change goals.

You are on a roll. Initially overwhelmed by the amount of time all of this activity takes, you feel that you have done a real bang up job.

Now you wait for those offers to just roll in. And you wait. And you wait—

Days go by, then weeks, then a month or more.

Nothing but silence—

At long last, the phone rings and a headhunter calls with a job opportunity, then another, then another. You are now busy with first interviews with the headhunter, the first interviews with the company, then second interviews, then third, then fourth then—nothing.

Days go by and—nothing.

Weeks go by and—nothing.

You have now experienced the nasty phenomenon called "cold weeks/hot days": periods of total silence followed by short periods of intense activity followed by additional periods of deafening silence.

Get used to it. This is normal. It is not personal. And, by the way, you cannot predict when it will start or stop.

You are not in control of the headhunter's or the potential new employer's time or priorities. You remember how it used to be when you were hiring people while trying to get the budgets finished and do several annual personnel reviews. Time goes by fast and priorities dictate that the job search will have to take a back seat to other more pressing matters. The result is that employers often don't have enough time to finish the search to help them out of the problem that created the need for the search.

Great news, huh!

Now that you realize what is happening. Get on with your search activities. Keep plugging away with the contacts and, guaranteed, that magic job will come.

Don't let it get to you. (And try to remember this when you start the hiring process in your next job. Remember the candidate out there waiting for your call.)

JOB HUNTING, COURTESY OF THE HUNTED

Remember what your mother said whenever someone (not a stranger) gave you a gift?

Say, "thank you".

The same holds true in the interview game, especially when you have had a face-to-face interview with the headhunter or the potential employer. Be sure to follow up your meeting with a short thank you note.

This gesture says a lot about your character and your professionalism.

All that is needed is a short concise note with a reference to the key point of the meeting. Don't brown nose and don't make the note a treatise on your industry knowledge.

Another tip: regardless of how long the headhunter or potential employer takes to respond to you, don't ever let their calls or questions linger on your "to do" list. Get back to them within 24 hours.

Whether this particular meeting or phone contact results in an offer for a job or not, the quality and timeliness of your response will be remembered for a long time afterwards. Word of mouth is a very powerful form of reference in job hunting. A poorly handled response can come back to haunt one many years later.

Lastly, learn how to smile over the phone. Your voice is often the first element of you that a potential employer comes in contact with. Upbeat, friendly voices are always a plus.

LIFE AFTER WORK

You will need to sit down while I share something with you.

THERE IS LIFE AFTER WORK!

Actually there are approximately 10-15 hours of free time in a day after work. This is often split between sleep, eating (need to cut down on this) and miscellaneous things like reading the paper, opening the mail and home repairs, things falling into the category of "other".

The "other" period is where most people waste a ton of time.

In my "other" time, I got an MBA. And through the entire time, I protested that I in no way had enough time to squeeze in a fulltime five-state sales territory, get my MBA, keep myself in shape and take part in family activities. It was embarrassing how much free time I carved out of my, supposedly too tight, schedule.

I know of one individual who was the mayor of a 120,000-person community in his spare time after his regular job of loading dock supervisor.

The point I am making is that we all have enough time to do anything we really want to do.

That is not the point of this essay, though it is a very important fact to recognize.

What is important to consider along with this "perceived tight time thing" is that balance in life is of utmost importance to your well being in your business life.

When someone says "get a life", they are probably telling you that you are totally out of synch with your life. You are being viewed as a workaholic. That is not a compliment. Being a workaholic is a clinical sickness and not a positive attribute.

The reason balance is so important today is that either you are presently out of a job or will be in the future. It is that other part of you (outside skills, other interests) that will help you get the next job or keep you sane while you go through the transition process.

When you get that next job, outside interests help recharge your batteries and give you a fresh perspective on life. Don't ignore it.

THE THEORY OF LOYALTY

Many theories abound in business.

I like one definition that I found in the dictionary for the meaning of "theory". This definition stated that "theory" was an explanation that has not yet been proven true, a guess or conjecture.

I would have to group the "Theory of Loyalty" into the pile of theories that either don't exist or maybe never existed, based on the litmus test of everyday business life.

Most of us grew up being taught that if we joined an organization, worked hard and gave the "company" 110%, we would be rewarded with a job for the rest of our lives. At one time in history and today, in many small family run or private companies, this work ethic still is practiced and supported. However, in virtually any public company, within any industry and regardless of size of organization, loyalty is now a one way street (from employee to employer). The other half of the equation (employer to employee) has disappeared in favor of the "company good" as defined by the "numbers" that will make Wall Street happy in the next quarter.

To drive this point home, decisions on closing operations, investing in R&D and in downsizing departments are being made solely on numbers, not on the basis of the impact on the people in the organization in question. Pick up any newspaper, any day, and this story is repeated.

So what does this mean to you?

Well, it means that you still have to put out your 110% for your present company but that you need to find another 110% to put into networking to get your next job lined up (inside or outside).

You must drive your own destiny, as you have never done before. Or else marry the bosses daughter (sometimes this doesn't work out either if you pick the wrong daughter).

The guarantees are gone, if there ever was such a thing.

You are now a permanent free agent.

Think like one. Plan like one. The gold watch after 20 years of continuous service is a vestige of the past.

OPTIONS, OPTIONS, OPTIONS!

You are out of a job and reading this book looking for that gem of an idea that will land your next job.

That is a good start.

And the news gets even better.

I GRANT YOU THE RIGHT TO DO ANYTHING YOU WANT TO DO!

I am not trying to be cute. I am only stating the obvious. You, as an individual, have the time and the choice to do with the rest of your life whatever you want to do.

In today's world, your options are literally unlimited:

Start a charity,

Return to a big business career,

Start your own at-home business,

Go into consulting,

Hitchhike around the world (or as one family named Nutts (true story) decided to do, they are going on a 3 year round the world cruise),

Write a book (hey I'm doing that myself)

Or buy a vineyard (something I am also investigating),

Buy a lotto ticket and fantasize,

Go back to school—

All of these options are doable by virtually every person reading this book. This "time out" in your career is a real opportunity to decide what you really want to do. This can be the chance to get out of the rut that you have been in since you went to work to live up to someone else's expectation of what you should be.

The bottom line is that you have unlimited options to go and do whatever you want.

So start today by putting together a list of what you like and what you are good at and see where this takes you.

Generate your own personal business plan.

Thoughts from the Other Side

Things sure look different when you're sitting on the other side of that decision desk.

You have no power.

You have no control over timetables.

You have no leverage to force things to happen.

It's damn humbling and frustrating.

No one returns phone calls. If they say they will get back to you in a certain time, the only certainty is that they won't.

And you can do nothing about it.

If nothing else, you reeeeaaaaly remember those who did call you, those who did admit that you were important enough to acknowledge.

Believe me, I will long remember those who treated me with dignity, something one feels a tad short of when one loses a job.

You never know where you will run into the same person again. Life is funny that way. You are almost guaranteed to run into the same person again that you dumped on, or who dumped on you. Exasperatingly, they normally are in a position where you reeeeaaaaly need them.

So try to remember all this when you do get your dream job. Try to remember what it was like on the other side of the desk.

SOUR GRAPES DON'T SELL

You have had your discussions with your manager and it is now official that you will not be attending the company picnic this year or the next—

You pack up your stuff, endure the stares from the survivors as you depart, saying goodbye to your close friends. I use this term rather loosely, as you will probably not hear from any of these people again. They will be wrapped up in their own survival tactics—no one wants to be guilty by association.

You are quickly out of sight and out of mind.

You return home and you're angry, very angry. You feel that the world has dumped on you and you don't like it. You want to tell the world about your anger and about that damn company that can't possibly survive without you (unfortunately, the survival instinct is pretty strong and most ex-companies not only survive but often prosper to your total frustration). But you just have to tell someone about all the negative things that your "ex" (this terms works for former employers just as well as for former marriage partners) did to the customers, to you, to the product and on and on.

When you get to the point of just exploding with anger and invective—STOP RIGHT THERE!

The worst thing you can do is carry out your personal war of retribution. It may feel good when you first blow off to anyone who will listen, but this explosion will have a long term negative effect on your reputation.

First off, most people (other than your wife who will unfortunately have to live up to that part of the marriage contract where the words

"for better or worse" are noted) don't want to hear a bunch of bad news and sour grapes. It's depressing and it's not funny.

They want funny and positive.

More importantly, no headhunter or potential employer wants to hear the bad news about a former company, as they cannot determine whether it was you or the company that was at fault. They really don't care to check it out. Your negative reference to a former employer does nothing but put a big black mark on your record. Your "potential employee" file is now terminated. You are carrying some "excess baggage" that they don't have any interest in taking on.

Get your anger vented by talking it out with your "for better or for worse" wife or husband, a professional counselor or by working it out with sports.

Avoid drinking it out as this is both expensive and doesn't work.

Believe me, it takes time, discipline and a loving, supportive family to help you get over it. But vent in private, not in public. This restraint will pay off big over the course of your life.

Life is too short to carry around all that excess baggage of bad memories.

TIME IS YOUR ALLY

Oh God! I have a severance package that is only good for X months (weeks, days)!

I must get a job in Y months (weeks, days) or I'm sunk!

Does this sound familiar?

Or, how about this? I'm 6 months into my severance package of 8 months and I have no offers. I have no choice but to grab at the first job that comes my way!

If you haven't experienced one of these situations yet, you probably will. Since you are in the elite level of the executive world with high salaries and plenty of perks that you hope to recover with the next job, your hunt will take approximately 1 month for each $10,000 of salary. In most cases, your severance will not cover this period of time.

Time to panic?

Not really. But definitely time to get your finances in shape. You have a goodly amount of staying power when you pool the credit limits on your credit cards, the equity in your home, your IRA or 401K program and stock investments. These funds will help you appreciate that you have the money to give you the time you need to find the RIGHT job.

The worst thing you could do is panic and jump into a job that isn't right for you. Not only would you probably be on the street in record time again but also this next job wouldn't give you much of a severance to cushion the blow. Then you would have 2 big strikes against you, a messy resume and weaker financial position.

The counterbalance to this concern of time working against you is the simple fact that time is working against your potential employer .

also. They need someone fast, though they don't seem to act like it. You are MR. RIGHT for some unknown job out there.

It takes time for the ultimate match to happen. And it will not be obvious where it may come from. I got one job from a want ad, one from my wife's tennis partner's husband, one from a retained search firm and another from a reference by a consultant to my former company.

To insure that you take the pressure off yourself, get a grip on your finances and plan for the worst case of 1 month in search time per $10,000 salary guideline I mentioned earlier.

Once this reality is understood and your finances are sound, a big load is taken off your back.

You can now devote yourself full time to landing the right job in record time.

THE NEXT STEP

It seems that today's market is a buyers market with 10 qualified candidates for every job opening. (The reverse of this is true for internet/e commerce jobs).

With this in mind, the interviewing process has become a marathon session where the employing company cannot get enough of seeing the wide range of high quality candidates. For them, it is like being a candy lover with enough money to buy any candy they want in the store. Part of the enjoyment seems to be in looking over all the many choices before deciding on the first candy type they saw when you walked in weeks, even months earlier. The thrill was as much in the hunt as in the final selection.

For we "sellees", this results in the game called "next step".

You are interviewed first by direct reports, then by indirect reports, then by peers of direct reports, then by those who will report to you. This process, when multiplied by the large number of candidates on the "first slate" or the "second slate", extends the process from days into months. You are qualified at each step to see if you will go to the next step.

High-speed technology has not yet hit the hiring process.

As a candidate, you are often not aware of whether you are even still being considered. Many times, the answer to your inquiries to a headhunter on this topic, are responded to with something to the effect that "the company is still evaluating different candidates and they will contact you when they reach a decision on the finalists". Weeks later, you may get a call saying that you are a finalist.

All too often, no call comes. Your follow-up call then results in finding out that the position has been filled weeks previous.

The only recommendation I can make to you to counter this frustrating reality is to be patient and to keep as many job hunts going as you can. Don't rely on a single promising lead to be the "one", thereby pushing off other job opportunities.

The hunt is not over until the paper is signed.

KEEP YOUR HEADLIGHTS ON HIGH

The DMV manual suggests keeping your headlights on high beam when driving on dark country roads or poorly lit streets to get full viewing of road conditions.

One should follow this advice when one drives his career. Eyes must be focused on the road for both the close-in problems and for the problems that are occurring down the road. In today's business climate, where the average career of a senior level manager is less than 3 years, you need to plan for this termination eventuality by building your worth inside your company, in your industry and within your network of philanthropic, church, charity, retained search and trade organizations.

Keep a close tab on the trends within your company as to its financial health and potential for it being acquired. Keep tabs on your industry for alternative technologies to obsolete your product. And keep the closest tabs on what is happening within your own organization as to what is "in" and what's "not in" with management in the areas of personnel promotions.

Being caught by surprise is no fun, especially when it is your job loss that is the surprise. Being in a position to drive rather than being driven puts you in control to determine your own future in your own timetable.

Keep those headlights on high!

CLOSING IN ON THE NEXT JOB

LEVERAGE LOST-DAY ONE

Do you know what takes place on the first day you join a new organization?

You immediately lose all your leverage!

Why do I mention this?

Only to emphasize the point that you have the greatest leverage during the job negotiation stage, but **prior** to signing on the dotted line. Once you sign, you are now the property of your new organization. It is bad form to try to change your employment agreement then. To try to change the agreement once on board, you can possibly even void your agreement. And you put a black mark in the great score book that is kept on all employees. Such second-guessing is a sure way to torpedo the company's trust in you.

So make sure that you think through what conditions you must have to reach a satisfactory agreement and then move ahead to get it. Once achieved, pat yourself on the back, sign the proposal and make a beeline to hitting the targets in your contract.

From now on your leverage will expand or contract in direct proportion to making your numbers and making your boss a success.

CONTRACTS-DON'T ASK/DON'T COMPLAIN

One of the best-kept secrets in business today is that you don't' have to be a President to be offered an employee contract.

Often, these agreements contain non-compete clauses, guaranteed severance payments (should another company acquire the hiring company or the job just doesn't work out for you or your employer) and guaranteed bonus/salary payments for the initial 1-2 years of the agreement.

Why would an employer want to give an employee a contract?

Several reasons come to mind:

>—**For the employee,** it gives security when a relocation is required or when a job is in a somewhat risky start-up company. Or, it is initiated to help bridge the earning gap that would occur when moving from one company to another between bonus periods.

>—**For the employer,** the contract is a way to lock in a key technical specialist or a senior manager for a critical position.

The further the job is from fitting these criteria, the less chance there is for any contract to be offered.

For both parties, the employment contract provides a level of security and commitment that is not provided by an offer letter alone. The contract can lock in a minimum term of employment, a guaranteed salary level and guaranteed bonus for the first partial fiscal period, stock options, reimbursement for specific milestones in a period of time and the all important exit severance package should the job situation not work out due to a change in company plans or your not fitting their needs. It is a very powerful and all encompassing document.

An employee contract is a device that protects you and your family from the somewhat whimsical management running companies today.

Investigate the company to find out whether contracts are offered either through the retained search contact handling this position or possibly from a friend in the company.

If the company offers such contracts, don't raise this issue until the offer stage. Sell yourself first. Then work out the best contract you can. Get legal help before signing to insure that you are properly protected.

DUE DILIGENCE

We do it when we buy houses.

We do it when we buy cars.

We do it when we buy clothes.

Amazingly, job hunters do little if any of it when we are looking for our next job.

What I am talking about is "Due Diligence", the conscientious investigation of a company before agreeing to hire on to this company.

What is the company culture-entrepreneurial or authoritarian, casual or regimented, stiff or convivial?

What new products are in the pipeline?

What is the competitive environment they are facing in each of their key markets?

What is their unique advantage and how is this protected-patents, know-how, and key technology gurus as founders?

Where is the company going in the industry-up or down? Why? What is the real financial picture of the company and how has it changed over the last 3 years? Why?

What is the background on the person you will be reporting to: Longevity, success in this industry, near retirement, on the short list for being fired?

What do the key customers think about this company and its products? Has this image changed over the last year, and, if so, in what direction and why?

What do the employees think of this company? What is the rate of employee turnover? Why is it so low or why is it so high? Both can be red flags of a problem.

Has your job been defined with a written job description or is it only verbally explained? Why?

The list could go on and on.

This next job is the one you hope to retire from. You are rolling the dice if you have little knowledge of what condition they are in and what directions they and their products and key people are going.

Your employment contract may give you some protections, but your goal is to have a good job not a good severance package and be back on the street. This means doing some real homework on your future employer. This job is made a lot easier with the Internet and the ability to tap into all of its data sources including the company's own website and those of relevant trade associations

Doing this homework is going to make your decision that much more educated and successful. It also may point up opportunities for you.

Take the time to do proper "Due Diligence" and you will have improved your job success by a substantial percentage.

THE COST OF MOBILITY

Quick job changes are another form of Russian Roulette.

I mean it.

Such changes are a sure way to make you a poor person with little time to recover.

Why? Let me give you a little historical perspective.

In the earlier part of this last century, one normally hired on for life in a particular business. You have probably read many stories of families where several generations of the family worked for the same company. The auto, steel and mining industries, banking and retail stores often come to mind.

As part of this hiring for the long term, many benefit packages were put into place for these long-term employees: health plans, retirement plans, IRA and, more recently, 401K plans. These programs had many nice features including company financial matching to employee contributions.

In these early retirement programs, vesting (earning ownership over the employer contribution) usually took 10 years. Vesting was an early form of employee retention The idea being that one could not afford to leave one company for another company since the money tied up in the vesting retirement program was so large and this money would be forfeited should an employee leave before vesting. This became known as the "Golden Handshake". Believe me, this device was a strong incentive to stay with a company in those days since options were not the norm.

Over the years, the vesting period dropped to seven years, then to 5 years and, more recently in the higher tech companies, to 3 years. This change in the vesting period had an interesting impact on employee career plans. When the economy was very stable and before merger

mania took off, one took the long view of working for a company for the minimum of the vesting period and normally for lifetime employment. Little real thought was given to leaving since the company provided so many benefits. The only exception being where one left voluntarily was for a very major promotion.

When merger mania took off and junk bonds helped accelerate the process, employee loyalty got thrown out the door. Employees were laid off in large numbers due to the mergers and they lost most, if not all, of their retirement benefits due to these layoffs. The government stepped in and tried to help alleviate the downside of such losses and to make companies pay for frivolous downsizing by lowering the vesting time period.

This government action did not stop the merger mania but, in fact, sped up employer decision making and awakened, in the employee, the realization that they no longer had the lifetime employment guarantee they thought they had, let alone the chance to get vested retirement benefits.

This was the beginning of the employee looking at himself as more of a "gun for hire". The cynicism of employees seeing companies buying and selling divisions and the resultant layoffs, led employees to expect that they would not get the vested benefits. Instead, a more viable option was to jump to new jobs for better titles and better immediate pay in the form of higher salaries and bonus payouts. Options started to be used as incentives. The days of blinding employee loyalty to their employers began to decline since, for all intents and purposes, the unspoken employer/employee loyalty bond had been broached by the employer.

The downside for many employees, who made these multiple moves between industries and between different companies, was that they had no portability of their benefits. Instead, they had to count on the increased compensation and the toys the higher compensation bought (especially housing, due to the relocation that was often required for these job jumps) to give them the foundation investments for their

retirement. This was a major shift from the company providing for employee retirement to that responsibility being thrust on the employee

For many people, this was a shift that worked greatly to their detriment.

Since they were shifting jobs quicker than the vesting period, little or no retirement benefits were vesting and the money they made in the new job often was used to cover the costs of the new home(often in more expensive regions of the country) and the hidden costs of getting settled into a new home. In addition, one has to then start the vesting period over again in the new company, which means losing tax breaks while you move into a new calendar year before you can join many of the programs (401K plans are a prime example).

They lost all of the contributed monies from their former employers, money that ran into the thousands of dollars from these forfeited plans. Over 30 plus years of leading this nomadic existence, these lost monies (when compounded by the accrued interest that would build up these nesteggs) added up to small fortunes being lost.

This does not even take into consideration the loss of industry expertise when switches occurred between industries. With a movement to a new industry, one became a rookie and had to earn his/her stripes again. So the leverage of tenure in an industry was also forfeited.

Sometimes these job changes were unavoidable due to an employee being made redundant as a result of a company merger or by the business going broke. However, many upwardly mobile employees made voluntary moves to "better their careers" and these were the most costly of all moves in the end.

So what am I saying?

DON'T VOLUNTARILY LEAVE YOUR JOB BEFORE YOU VEST IN BOTH YOUR RETIREMENT AND STOCK OPTION PLANS.

ONLY MAKE THE MOVE FOR A REALLY GREAT JOB!

Cover such an accelerated vesting approach in your contract, if possible, should this be an involuntary departure.

Beyond that, I support the move underway to give employees full portability of benefits when moving from one job to another. I also strongly suggest that companies who lay off personnel must be forced to vest that person immediately in at least 50% of the those retirement plans or options that would have been vested fully should this person have been willing to stay on for the full vesting period. These are things that you need to make your congressman aware of.

As it stands now, this forfeited option/retirement money is like a hidden reserve account for the employer.

For those of you in your first transition, this essay is meant to be a jolt of reality that you need to think about before joining your next company and, definitely, before leaving the next company.

Know what you are losing and do the math. For those who are chasing the e-commerce .com game with its insane hours and the promise of untold wealth once your company goes public, recognize that over 75% of these companies will not survive and the options will either go underwater or disappear with the folding or absorbed company. In the meantime, your body and bank account will be the worse for the wear.

Look before you leap. The cost of mobility is substantial.

SECTION 4

AFTER THOUGHTS

Job Hunting, Courtesy of the Hunter

I put this section in to get something off my chest as well as to remind myself not to be an insensitive clod when I do get my next job.

One in search of a job, after the trauma of a general layoff or a firing, has his/ her morale at the bottom of the well and his/her self-esteem equally in the pits. The last thing they want to be is ignored.

One minute they were controlling a million-dollar budget and 50 employees with people jumping when they asked for things to get done. They were dedicated employees used to working on tight schedules and those working for them were used to working to those same schedules.

The next minute, the authority is gone. Just that fast, they are a pariah.

This diatribe is not intended for those of you going through the search. Instead, it is aimed at those headhunters and potential employers of the world who claim to be looking for the right person to drive their company to new sales records while showing superhuman abilities to raise employee morale, increase productivity and elevate loyalty to new heights.

You (headhunter and potential employer) are giving all the wrong signals to the potential employee during the hiring process.

With all that said, let me suggest a few simple rules for handling job candidates, recognizing that most of us will be a candidate in the future.

1) If you place an ad for a job, state in the body of the ad that a reply will be forthcoming within X number of days (30 days is more than reasonable to filter through the pile of resumes). Replies should go to both those qualified and those not qualified to bring closure to the unqualified candidate and to provide some form of next step timing to those still being considered.

2) When you state a date for follow up, follow up by that date. It is reverse water torture waiting for the call that never comes. Understand that candidates have lives too. In fact, they are adjusting their schedules to meet your deadlines. Yanking them around with sloppy follow up breeds contempt even for your best candidate.

3) If you have voice mail, then respond to your messages within a reasonable time (max of 48 hours). Have your secretary answer for you if your schedule doesn't allow for you to respond. Just respond.

4) If a search has been cancelled or delayed in which a candidate has been involved as a finalist, let he or she know this has happened along with the cause of the delay or cancellation.

5) By all means treat people with common courtesy and respect. It costs no money, but the "free press" from positive communication spreads like wildfire.

What a Difference 4 Years Makes!

While I wrote many of the sections of this book starting 4 years ago (during my last right of passage through the "transition" zone), the change in technology since then has been so dramatic that one can almost enjoy the process just because of the new technological tools.

Now we have high speed PC's (I wrote on an AST 25 meg machine), the Internet, scanners and high speed printers. Now, there is no need to go down to Kinkos with one's clumsily typed resume and spend several hours and cost oneself "an arm and a leg" picking out the paper, type style and format before buying 1000 copies of the retyped resume and the envelopes for mailing them out.

Hey, you can design your own resume in any format and type you want (all automatically spell checked and properly blocked). And, you can e-mail the whole kit and kaboodle (I just can't get away from using the old time slang that I grew up with in Indiana) to anyone with a single keystroke.

No manual addressing of envelopes and making the postal service rich on the postage (and, I might add, ticking off the local mailman with the overstuffed mailbox of resumes you thrust on him daily). In fact, your whole search takes place in complete privacy. No mailman, no UPS driver and no neighbors are made aware of your activity.

Your cover is blown, however, by coming out for the morning paper at 10AM unshaven in the middle of the week.

There are some neat tricks that I found in my most recent "sabbatical". One trick relates to mass e-mailing to your key contacts or retained search list. This chore can be done simply by listing one name in the "to" address with the remainder of the contacts in the "bcc"

address area. The "bcc" acts as an individual mailing to each person on the list rather than appearing as just a "dear occupant" mass mailed memo. Another trick is to send out these mailings every other month as it keeps your name current in the eyes of the retained search firms whose turnover in jobs makes resumes obsolete daily.

For those of you who have not yet signed up for your own e-mail address, it is a very simple 5-10 minute exercise. The power unleashed having a connection to the Internet is unobtainable anywhere else. It is a must to have.

"Voila"! Now that you have the fully loaded PC and home office set up including the Internet connection, you are fully ready to get the word out that you are a free agent. With the power of the new software programs, you can also pursue a parallel existence as a new business entity with your own professionally done calling cards. (Hallmark, among others make great software to do anything fancy you want done).

So, today, you are more in control of your destiny than ever before. Between Monster.com job postings and retained search sites with additional job postings, you can do most searching for new jobs, company backgrounds and sundry information from that little office in your own home. No more trips to the libraries. Much of your office expenses may even be tax deductible.

The difference in 4 years lies in the tools.

However, networking remains the best form of finding the next job. Some things never change.

Mosquitoes and High Tech Employment

I see an interesting analogy between mosquitoes' attraction to bright lights especially candles, bug zappers and campfires and being an employee in a high technology company.

Both eventually end in termination.

What is most attractive to the mosquito ends up killing him. The similar result holds true for those who are in high tech. They are drawn to the magnetic attraction of the fast paced Promised Land of big money and even bigger stock options. All too often they end up on the street after the technology failed, the company was bought out or downsized due to the "market not right for this product yet" or the plain fact that some technologies just don't have a large enough market to support them.

Or even worse, they trash themselves physically with the insane hours to get a hopeless product to market.

If you are one of these people (the fatally technically drawn), you should use your resume as a screen saver on you PC since you will be updating it so often.

It is a fact of your life that you will well exceed the historical average of 6 job changes in your lifetime. In e-commerce, having this many different jobs in a 2-year period is not only not far fetched but almost a "red badge of courage" and "right of passage" in Silicon Valley. One needs to fail at least once to get one's ticket punched and prove oneself worthy of having "industry experience".

For those in this category, this book is not for you since you seem to thrive on job change with little concern for the transition process. However, should you have bought this book to read during one of your

"all nighters", you might want to review the essay on "The Cost of Mobility" again. This essay speaks directly to the potential fate you will face with all of these job changes.

I would also strongly recommend having your friends invest in a good psychologist to be put on retainer to mentor you through this fickle career path.

Good Luck!

PERCEPTION IS REALITY

How many times have you seen peers or friends get credit for doing a great job that they had little or nothing to do with?

Aggravating as this is, it happens all the time. The hardest worker or the most loyal employee or the most creative personality gets little recognition and even less credit for their contribution to the overall success of the company.

This phenomenon is best explained by the phrase "Perception is Reality".

This phrase is a fundamental tenet of good marketing. In this case though, we are not talking about a product but about your image in the new or old company.

Don't hide your accomplishments.

You need to make sure that people know what you are doing to be able to judge your relative value. The more others are aware of your accomplishments and your efforts, the larger your image in the organization and the more your value grows in proportion to your peers. Over time, this expanding of your image results in a perception that you are actually doing more than you may be doing. Nothing wrong with this halo effect, since "perception is reality".

I talk not of sucking up or grandstanding, both of which will get you low marks with your boss and your peers. I am merely saying that you must be your own best PR agent since no one has been officially assigned this task.

Being successful in this ability will prove invaluable when the new job opens up, the annual salary review rolls around or the inevitable downsizing plan is initiated.

You will be on the "A" list for the good things and on the "do not touch " list for the bad things.

Epilogue

Now that you have read through this book, let's go out and attack those mountains but this time with a more balanced view of the world around you and your own capabilities!

Life is too short to carry around all that baggage from the last job, so close that chapter on that book and ceremonially trash it.

Good Luck!

ABOUT THE AUTHOR

Michael T. McCraley was born and grew up in South Bend, Indiana. He graduated from Purdue University in West Lafayette, Indiana with his BS in Industrial Management and from Xavier University in Cincinnati, Ohio with his MBA in Marketing.

He has spent over 25 years working in the Beverage, Semiconductor, Industrial Automation and Printed Circuit Board Fabrication industries where he held senior management positions in sales, marketing and operations. He has worked for American companies (American Can, Newport Corporation, Control Automation, Unimation, and Excellon Automation) and Japanese companies (Seiko Instruments and Panasonic). His worldwide experience entailed responsibility for subsidiaries in Europe and the Pacific Rim in addition to his North American duties.

With this breadth of experience and time in the markets noted, Michael has had the dubious and first hand distinction of experiencing the cyclical ups and downs of these industries from which this book got its beginnings.

This is Michael T. McCraley's first book though he has written and had published numerous articles in trade journals as well as business and personal newsletters. In addition, he has made formal presentations in the United States, Europe and the Pacific Rim on Industrial Automation.

He lives with his wife, Marla, in Rolling Hills Estates, California using what free time he has to immerse himself in his hobbies of jogging, reading, wine tasting and woodworking.

www.ingramcontent.com/pod-product-compliance
Lightning Source LLC
Chambersburg PA
CBHW030802180526
45163CB00003B/1140